Remembering Agra

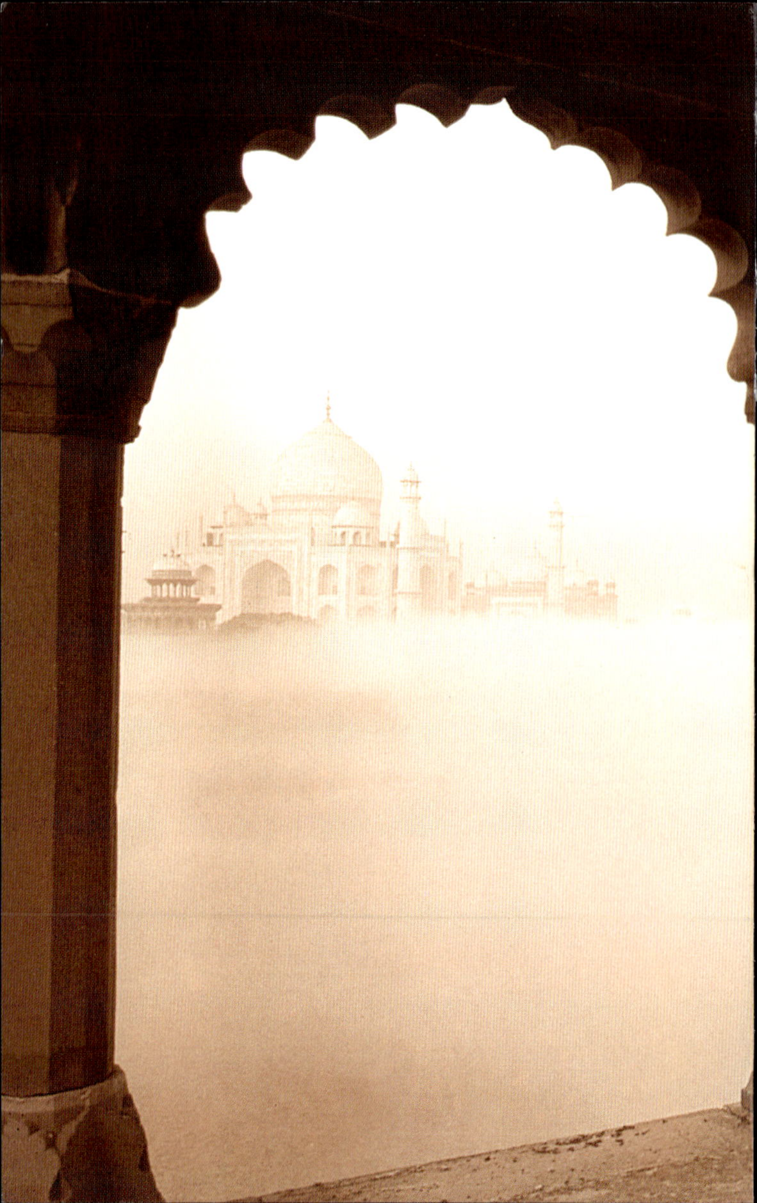

Remembering Agra

TEXT

Shailaja Kathuria

PHOTOGRAPHS

Victoria & Albert Museum, London

Lustre Press
Roli Books

It is traditional to make playful speculations on the etymology of the name of a place. It was believed by some that Agra was derived from the Hindi word *agar,* used to describe the brackish soil of this region. Others thought that the city got its name from the Agarwal *banias,* who inhabited this place in large numbers. Agra could also simply mean *age-rah* – the way ahead.

'The way ahead' – it certainly turned out to be for Babar. However, one must not forget his predecessor, Sikandar Lodi, who seems to have been the first emperor to make Agra his capital. He is also remembered for leaving his name on what later became an important suburb of Agra – Sikandra. He built a small *barahdari* or pavilion there in 1495, which was converted into a tomb for Mariam Begum, one of Akbar's wives. Akbar's mausoleum itself stands in the very same Sikandra.

If one were to enter Agra by boat on the Yamuna and go downstream, one could literally see 'the way ahead' and its symbols in the form of Babar's gardens, Akbar's fort and finally, Shah Jahan's Taj Mahal.

It is interesting to note that the Agra of Sikandar Lodi and Akbar stood on the right or western bank of the Yamuna, and that of Babar and Humayun on the opposite bank. When Babar occupied Agra in 1526, he is believed to have founded a new ward in the city, nostalgically christened Kabul. The implication is obvious. He wanted to stay on and make Agra his home. Stay on he did; though nothing more is known of the elusive Kabul! It is possible that all the gardens he laid out (on the left bank of the river) like the Chahar Bagh, the Achank Bagh and the Zahara Bagh formed a part of this Kabul. Gardens had been a favourite with Babar's Timurid ancestors and remained so with his descendants. It is likely that Babar built some fortifications on the left bank of the river. It is almost certain that a fort seems to have been built on the same ground as Akbar's.

Remains of this fort, which was 'replaced' by Akbar's, have been found.

A structure relating to Sher Shah Suri's time is the tomb of Alawal Balawal in the Nai ki Mandi quarter of the city with which an amusing anecdote is associated. The tomb is of an Arab Saint, Saiyyad Alauddin, who came to Agra during Sher Shah's reign. There is a legend that one of Sher Shah's camel-drivers had (with his master's consent but in defiance of the Saint's expostulations) stabled his camels in the mosque. The building began to sink until it crushed the camels and did not stop until the Saint cried, 'Enough!' With this the Surs themselves sank into oblivion and in their place returned one of the most celebrated of Babar's descendants, Akbar.

It was the Agra Fort or Akbarabad (as it came to be known later) that symbolised the flowering of the Mughal imperial culture in Agra. Akbar turned his attention to building after having politically consolidated his position. Abul Fazal in the *Akbarnama* gives an account of the foundation of modern Agra by Akbar. 'His Majesty made Agra, the capital of his Empire and . . . took up his residence in the citadel formerly known as Badalgarh . . . the city within a short time became an ornament of the seven climes. It is a city possessing a salubrious climate . . . The soil is congenial to the growth of the trees and fruit of Khorasan and Iraq . . . The river Jún (Jumna) . . . flows in the midst of the city. On either side of it the nobles and servants of the State have constructed edifices of such beauty and elegance that they surpass description.'

Fatehpur Sikri and the Agra Fort were completed in 1571. The *Diwan-i-Am* of the Agra Fort was the hall of public audience, where Akbar held court, administered justice, issued orders and met with the chiefs of Hindustan and envoys from foreign lands. It is ironic that centuries later the British were to adopt the grand Mughal durbar first held there as a symbol of gaining legitimacy among the Indian rulers and their subjects.

From the imperial court of the *Diwan-i-Am* and the houses of the nobles into the *mohallas* of Agra flowed a culture that was to become a part of the life of the people and a fashion for many of the smaller chiefs of India to emulate. In this were included many of the favourite sports of the Mughal emperors such as *chaugan*, a game similar to polo, chess, elephant fights and pigeon-keeping. In Agra the already popular Braja sports of wrestling and swimming found patronage among the Mughals.

The celebrated Agra *gharana* (school) of music was one of the shining examples of Mughal patronage which originated in Akbar's time. Sujan Singh, one of Akbar's Rajput *sipah salars* (military officers), is said to be its founder and an early exponent of *Dhrupad*. In more recent times, the Agra *gharana* has produced such fine artists as Ustad Faiyyaz Khan and Ghaghe Khuda Baksh.

Another kind of local art, which still continues to flourish, was first patronised by Akbar and then extensively by Shah Jahan. This is the craft of stone inlay, particularly in marble.

It is significant that the pavilions of the Angoori Bagh in the Fort were some of the few pre-Shah Jahan Mughal structures to be built exclusively in marble. The Angoori Bagh was laid out in front of the Khas Mahal by Akbar and intended for the use of his harem.

The other such building was the garden tomb of Itmad-ud-daula (Ghiyas Beg) across the river. The whole structure is of white marble inlaid with coloured stones. Itmad-ud-daula was a Persian adventurer from Tehran who went on to become Jahangir's *wazir* (prime minister), and was the father of the Empress Noorjahan. It was she who completed this exquisite building. It is said that at first she had proposed that the mausoleum be built of solid silver but was wisely dissuaded by the architect on the ground that it would inevitably attract thieves. He thus saved Itmad-ud-daula from being seen and remembered for its opulence rather than for its delicate beauty.

Akbar's mausoleum at Sikandra was started during his lifetime but completed by Jahangir in 1613. It is a magnificent structure in red sandstone surrounded with extensive gardens and a lofty gateway. It is curious that as opposed to the prevailing Islamic custom, which required the dead person's face to be turned in the direction of Mecca, Akbar's corpse was placed with his head to the west, facing east. But then Akbar was well known for his experiments with religious syncretism while he was on the throne and his final resting position is just another example of his secular thinking.

Another lesser-known but important example of Akbar's legacy of curiosity about other faiths and his generosity towards them is that he made Agra home to one of the oldest Roman Catholic missions in the country. A grant of land was made by him in Mauza Lashkarpur (now Ghatia Azam Khan) in the mid-sixteenth century and a church was built there. It was burnt down during Jahangir's reign, but rebuilt by Begum Samru in 1769.

In spite of his personal intimacy with his grandfather, Shah Jahan did not seem to have taken lessons in religious tolerance. He, however, did inherit Akbar's aesthetics on building and carried forward and greatly embellished his style.

No king used marble on the scale that Shah Jahan did. Among Shah Jahan's buildings in the Fort, one of the grandest is the Moti Masjid or the Pearl Mosque, completed in 1653. It is made entirely of white marble and was built to accommodate large gatherings.

The other congregational mosque built in Agra at this time was the Jami Masjid. Although started during Shah Jahan's time, it was endowed extensively by his daughter, Jahanara. It is built in red sandstone and is situated immediately outside the Fort. Its grand gateway was pulled down by the British during the Mutiny in 1857.

These buildings were constructed about the same time as the most celebrated of Mughal monuments, the Taj Mahal. By the time the building of the Taj was completed, the imperial court had moved from Agra to Delhi. But on its completion, as on that of other prominent buildings, Shah Jahan made a special visit to Agra to survey the Taj. For Shah Jahan personally, it was much more than a poignant symbol of his love for Mumtaz; it was the culmination of imperial and architectural grandeur.

By the 18th century, the Taj was being noticed and admired by European travellers, artists and others; but Agra was seen as a sad heap of ruins. It is ironic that as the Taj was gradually becoming a legend, the absence of a 'high culture' in Agra led to the city being neglected and it was difficult to comprehend how the imperial, beautiful and almost celestial Taj Mahal belonged to Agra!

Oh friends, that Tajganj which stands here
Whose fame is spread far and wide
Whose beauty and perfection one cannot doubt
In whose quarter is the shrine that stands by the river,
And that too is of the most unusual beauty
Whose praises I cannot stop singing, O Nazir,
It is my daily occupation.

Nazir Akbarabadi in *Tajganj ka Rauja*

In stark contrast to the dirge sung by European travellers, Nazir's poems speak of a robust, bustling town. Although the beauty and perfection of the building did not go unnoticed by Nazir, he spoke of the Taj Mahal as principally being a *mazhar* or a shrine. In fact, till the time the entrance to the main graves was blocked off a few years ago, one could always see people lighting lamps and praying there.

It is believed that the Tajganj bazaar or Mumtazabad (as it was commonly referred to earlier) was part of the Taj complex. Indeed you do get a feeling of walking in from a vast courtyard into the corridor of a home, especially when you enter the bazaar from the west gate of the outer courtyard of the Taj. You can walk to Malikon ki Gali in Tajganj where Nazir lived, and through Resham Katra and Purani Mandi to Kinari Bazaar. It is here that Nazir used to join the procession on Holi and go forth towards the older *mohallas* of Mandi Said Khan, Nai ki Mandi, Shahganj and Gokulpura.

Several of his poems are descriptions of local festivals and activities which still take place in the Brajbhoomi region. Kanhaiyaji ka Janam, Baldevji ka Mela, Agre ki Tairaki, Basant and Holi are a few. Wrestling was and still is a star attraction at any Braj fair and Nazir's *Aabroo aur Tandrusti* extolled the virtues of fitness and good health as vital to the personality of an honourable man. Wrestling found patrons among local British officials and princes alike. Agre ki Tairaki in particular was an immensely popular Yamuna swimming festival that was held during the monsoons. Nazir writes about it with great spirit:

When arrives the season of the swimming fair,
Then come the high-spirited of Agra to swim there,
So do the restless and those who are patient,
With them swim the innocent and the novices,
The accomplished and the mature,
So do the old and the young,
The petty, the poor, the penniless and the rich,
In this Agra, O what stalwart swim.

Nazir Akbarabadi in *Agre ki Tairaki*

There was nothing that gave Nazir and his friends joy that he did not write about. One of his poems is devoted entirely to a favourite edible - *til ke laddoo* - a sweet made from sesame seeds. Had Nazir lived for a few more decades he would surely have written metres of verse with the same pride and joy on the famous Agra *petha* – a sweet made from pumpkin. Certainly the oldest *halwai* or confectioner in the city, Bhimsain Baijnath's shop was set up in 1865 in Kinari Bazaar. It claims to be the first *petha* maker. It is believed that the *petha* is effective in the treatment of jaundice and other liver ailments.

Nazir's poems are not to be dismissed as frivolous outbursts. Their importance lies in dispelling the stereotypes of a post-Shah Jahan 'dark age' in Agra - the stereotype of the Taj being the only gleaming pearl in a city of darkness, of it being trapped like a hapless angel in the midst of a coarse and backward culture. Nazir showed the way; the way into the brightness of the *mohallas* and *mandis* of Agra; the way into the heart of Agra of which the Taj was a part. Just as the Yamuna tied the kings' cities together, so did the Taj Mahal tie the king-city to the peoples' city.

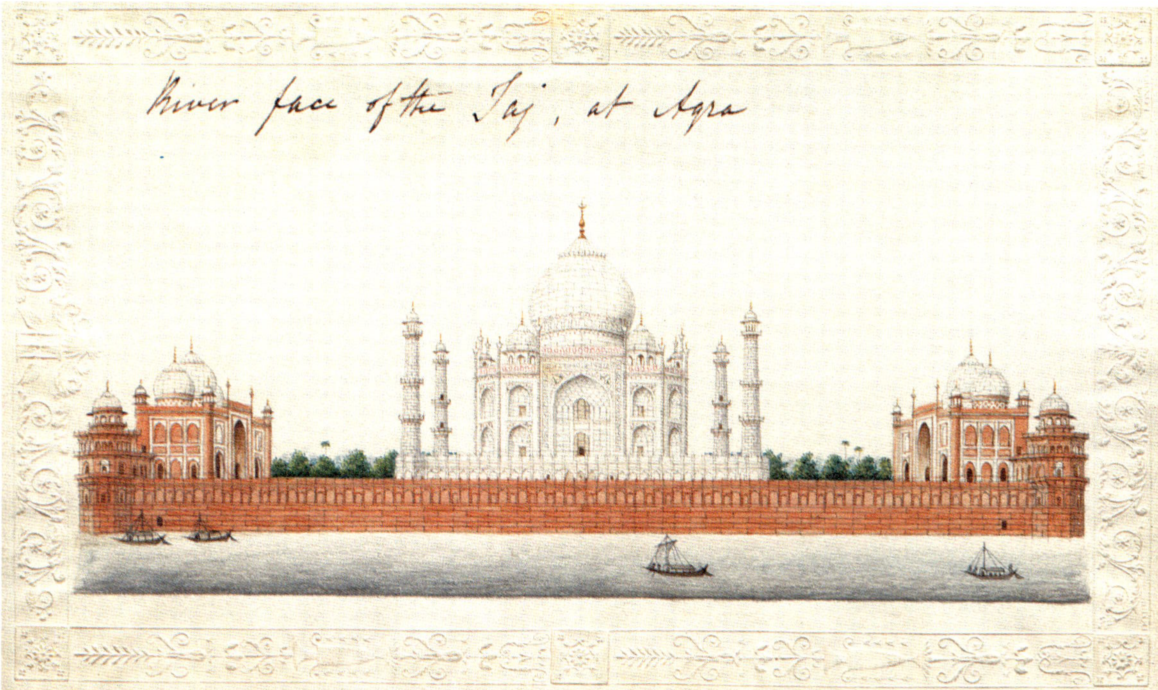
River face of the Taj, at Agra

■ River face of the Taj at Agra, c. 1643

Shah Jahan always entered the Taj from the riverside – coming by boat from the Agra Fort – possibly in a barge similar to the ones in the picture. Many 18th-century English visitors to Agra would also take the river route and view the Taj from the Yamuna and some from across it.

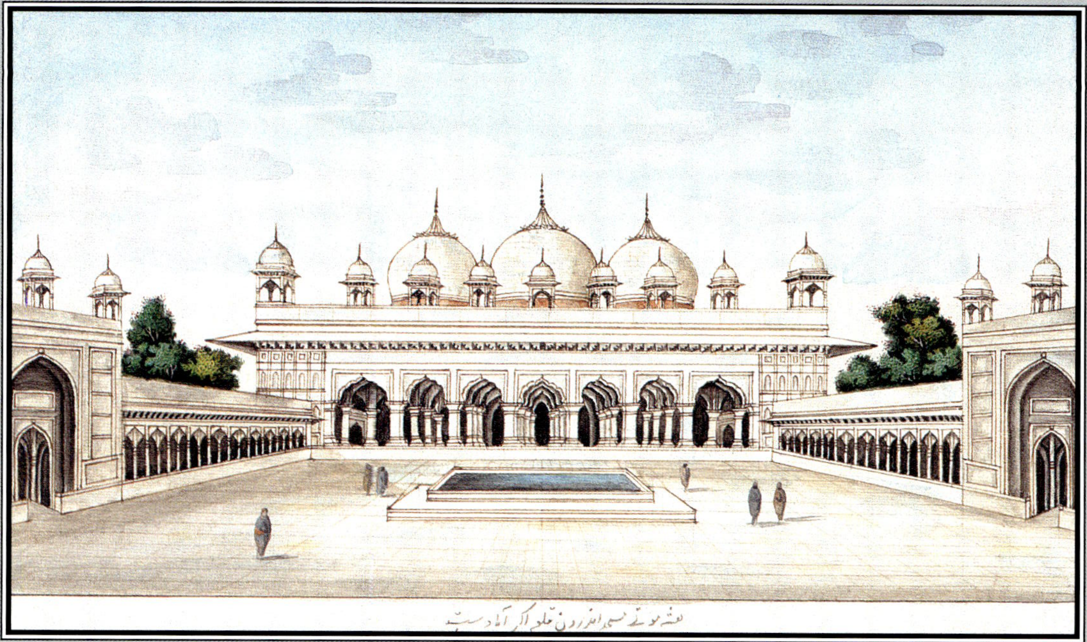
نقشه موتی مسجد اندرون قلعه اکبرآباد است

■ The Moti Masjid, Agra, c. 1653

This was one of Shah Jahan's additions to the Fort of Agra and in the tradition of the Taj Mahal (it was built soon after the latter's completion). it is made entirely of marble. The purity of its form and architectural perfection of its building stand out due to its restrained ornamentation. Sleeman wrote, 'There is no mosaic upon any of the pillars or panels of this mosque; but the design and execution of the flowers in the bas-reliefs are exceedingly beautiful.'

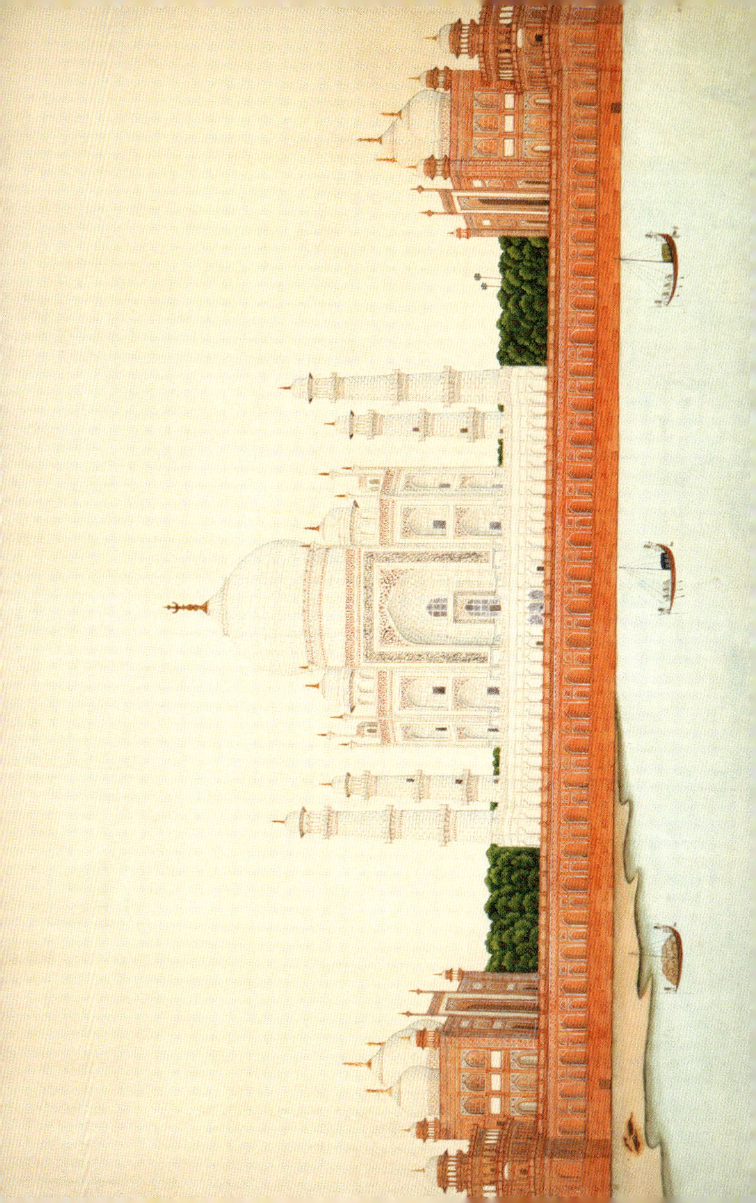

■ The Taj – view from the river, c. 1643

The Agra stretch of the Yamuna has a unique significance in that, on its banks, lie the most impressive remains of the cities of the four Mughal emperors. In a real as well as symbolic way, the Taj Mahal is (going downstream) the last and greatest building.

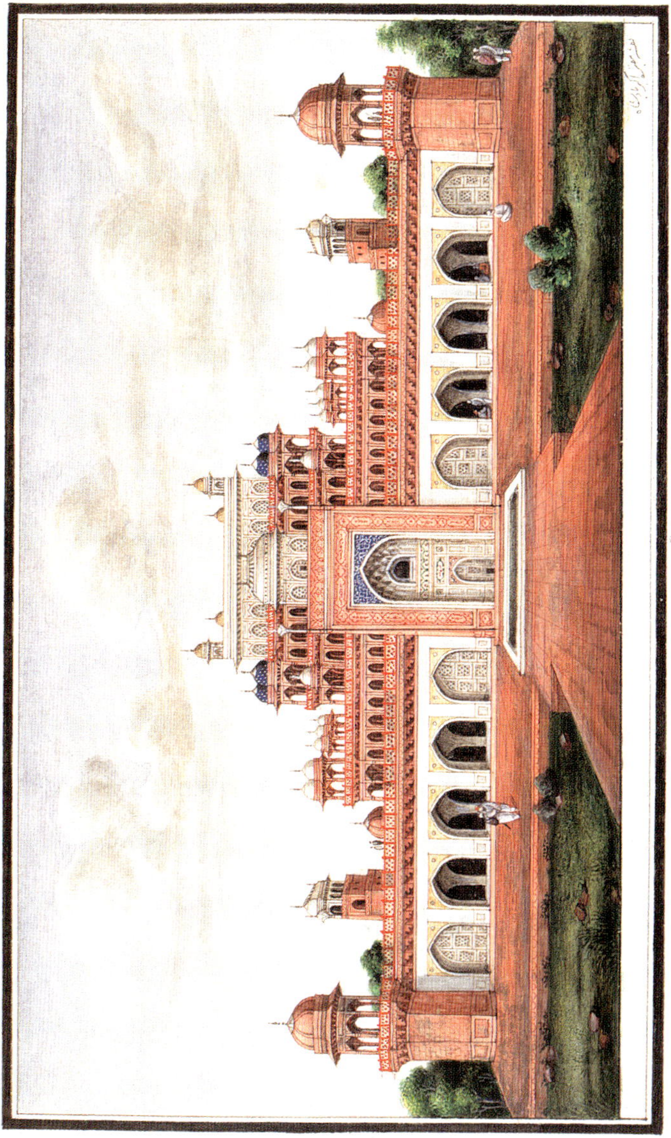

■ Akbar's mausoleum, Sikandra, c. 1610

This was begun by Akbar during his own lifetime and completed by his son, Jahangir. Though set in a typical Mughal tomb garden, it is most unusual in its design of a terraced pyramid. It is completely unlike his predecessor, Humayun's mausoleum at Delhi, and the Taj Mahal, built later, which were more in the Timurid tradition of domed tombs.

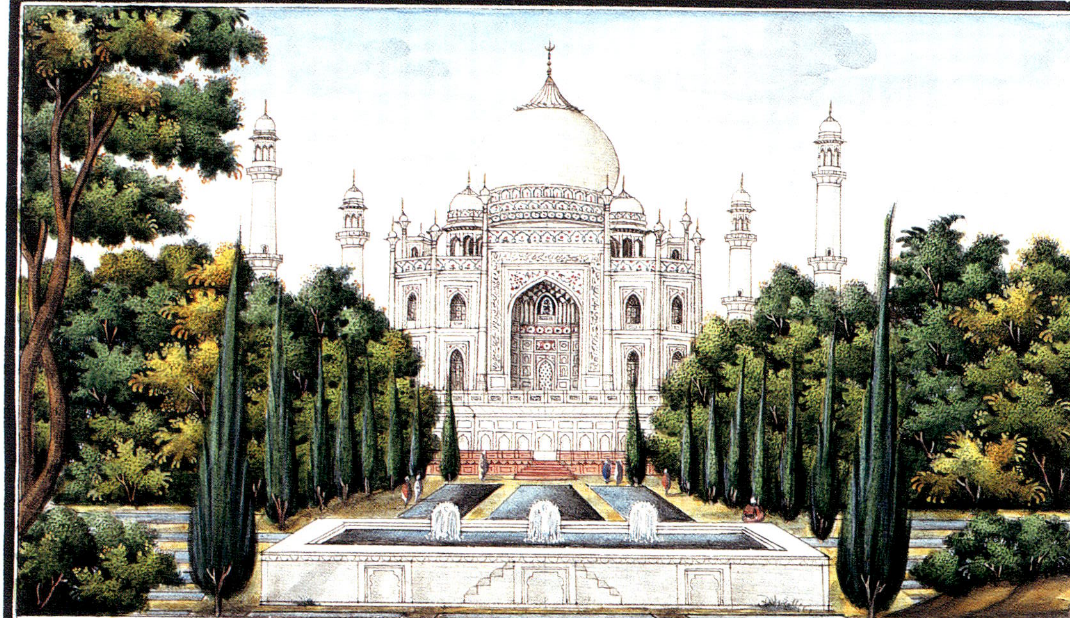

■ The garden view of the Taj Mahal, c. 1643

The depiction of the Taj with an overgrown garden before it, somehow made it seem less formal than what it looks like today, and much more a part of the whole complex of the mazhar *(shrine), garden and bazaar as it was first conceived. The bazaar of Mumtazabad or Tajganj (as it is known today) was set up to foster a feeling of closeness to the mausoleum among the people of Agra and in a more practical way, to raise revenue for its maintenance.*

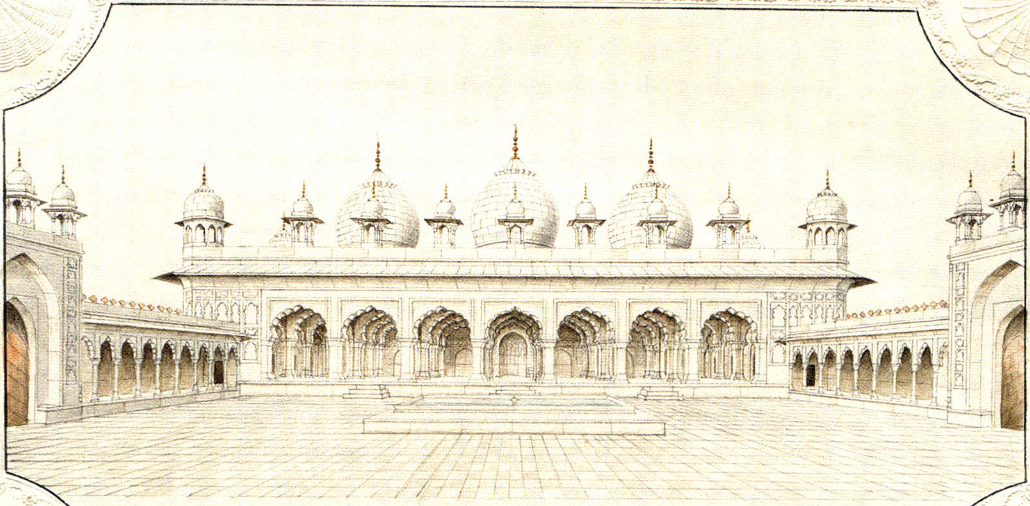

Motee Musjid, or Pearl Temple, in the Fort at Agra

■ The Moti Masjid, Agra, c. 1653

Other than the beauty of its form, the Moti Masjid's uniqueness lies in its being the largest of the three Pearl Mosques built by Shah Jahan and the only one intended for a full Friday congregation. The ones in Delhi and Lahore were quite small, built mainly for use of the royal family.

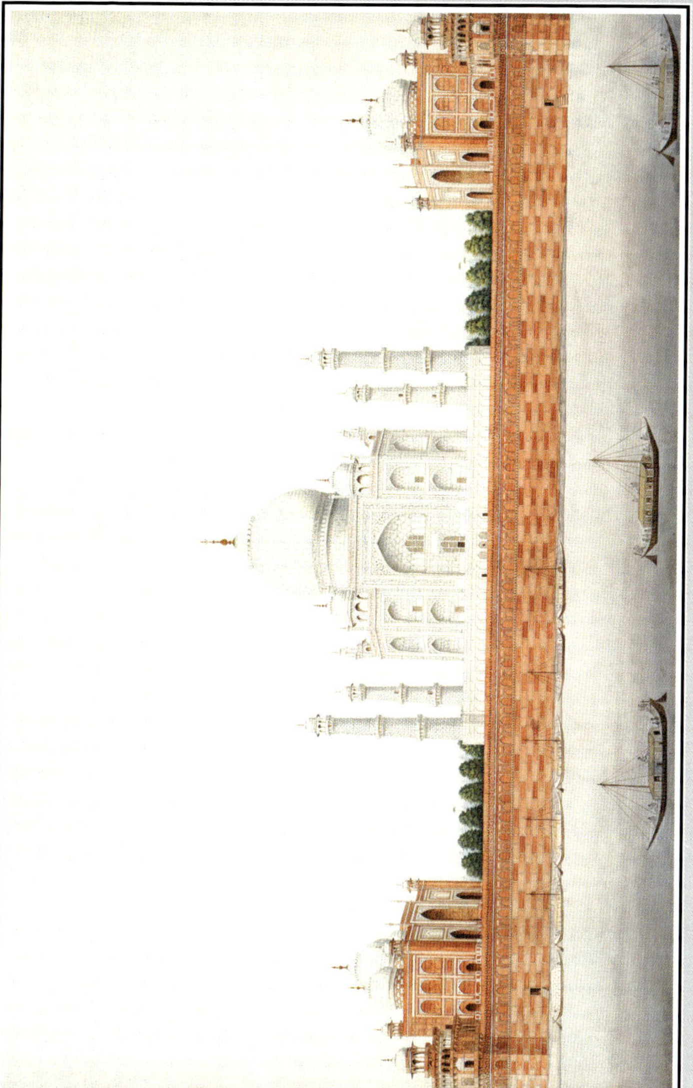

■ The Taj – a closer view from the river, c. 1643

In most indigenous accounts of the Taj, like in those of the local poet Nazir's poems, the mausoleum is never described without a mention of it being located on the banks of the Yamuna. This was because it was not seen as an isolated monument, but as a mazhar *or shrine close to the hearts of the people of Agra. It was thus as sacred to them as was the river Yamuna.*

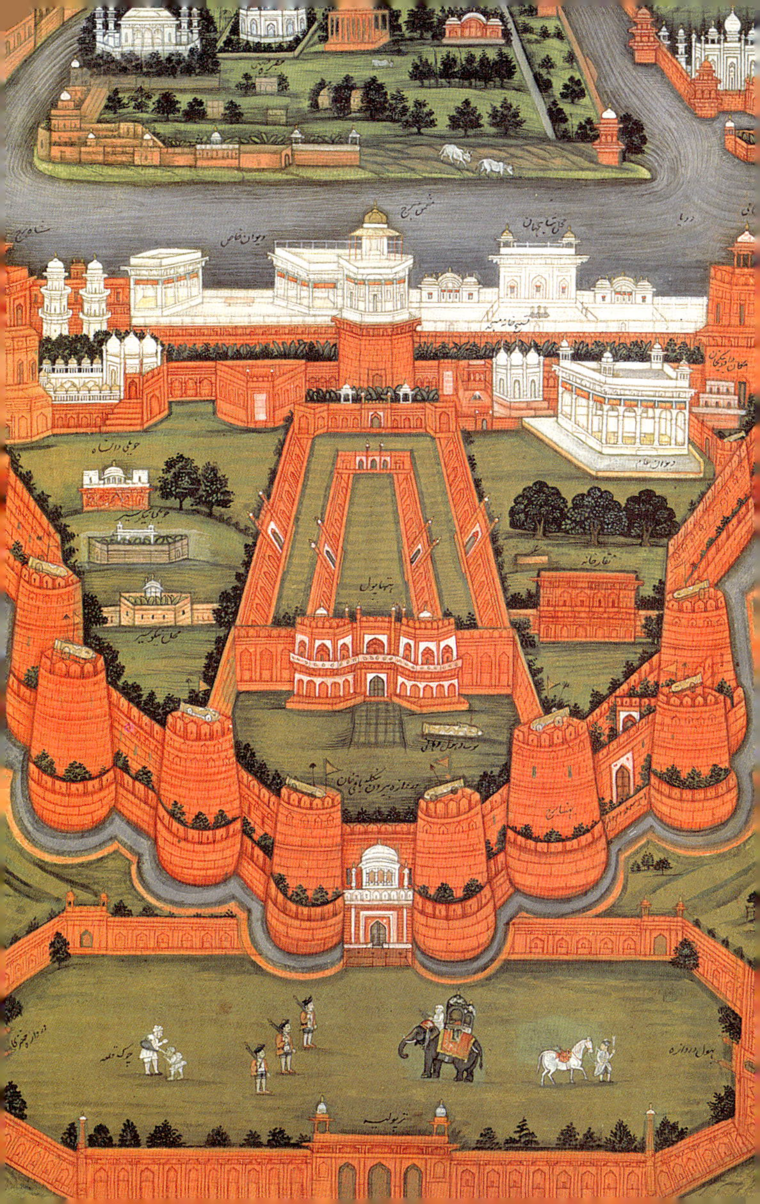

دیوان عام
نقارخانه
ترپولیه
دریا

■ Agra Fort, c. 1571

Though later added to by Jahangir and Shah Jahan, the Red Fort at Agra was first built by Akbar and aptly christened Akbarabad, marking the formal founding of the Mughal Empire in India. Architecturally it marked the beginning of the tradition of the sandstone-marble combination. When Akbar decided to build the city of Akbarabad he gave an order that his palaces should be made of copper. But he was politely dissuaded by his wise architect. Thus he built his palaces and fortress of red hewn stones of great size.

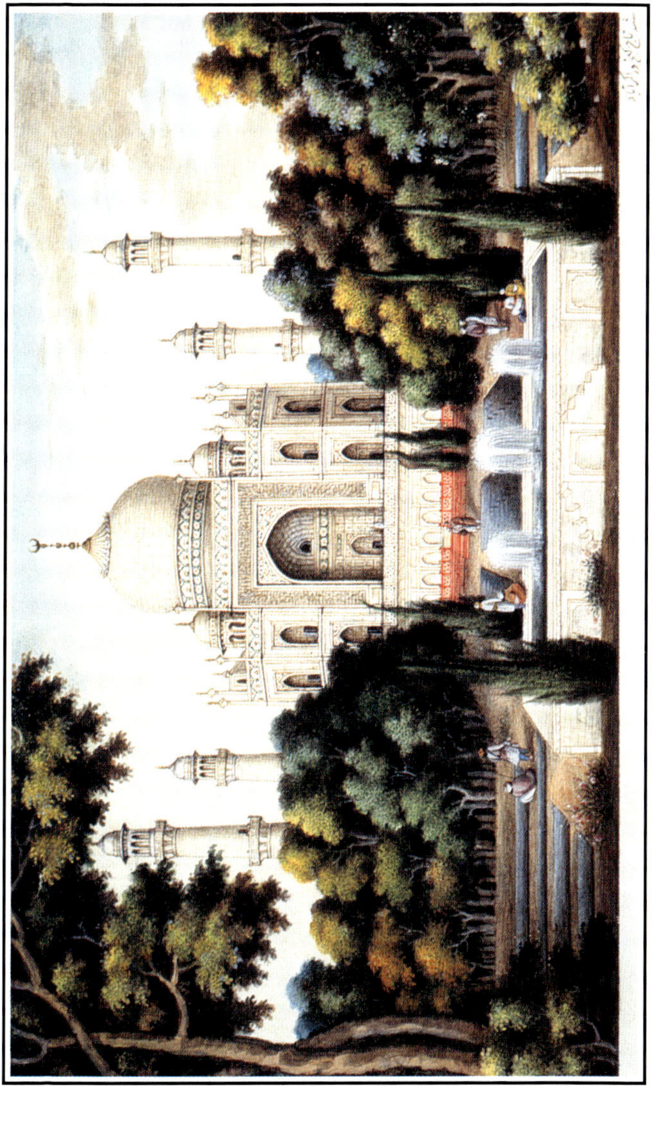

■ Garden view of the Taj Mahal, c. 1643

The garden view of the Taj Mahal is today the most classic depiction of the building. What gives it this spectacular perspective is the fact that unlike most other Mughal garden tombs, the Taj Mahal lies at one end of the garden and not in the centre. Moreover, the water channels here are wider and thus heighten the 'garden of paradise' effect.

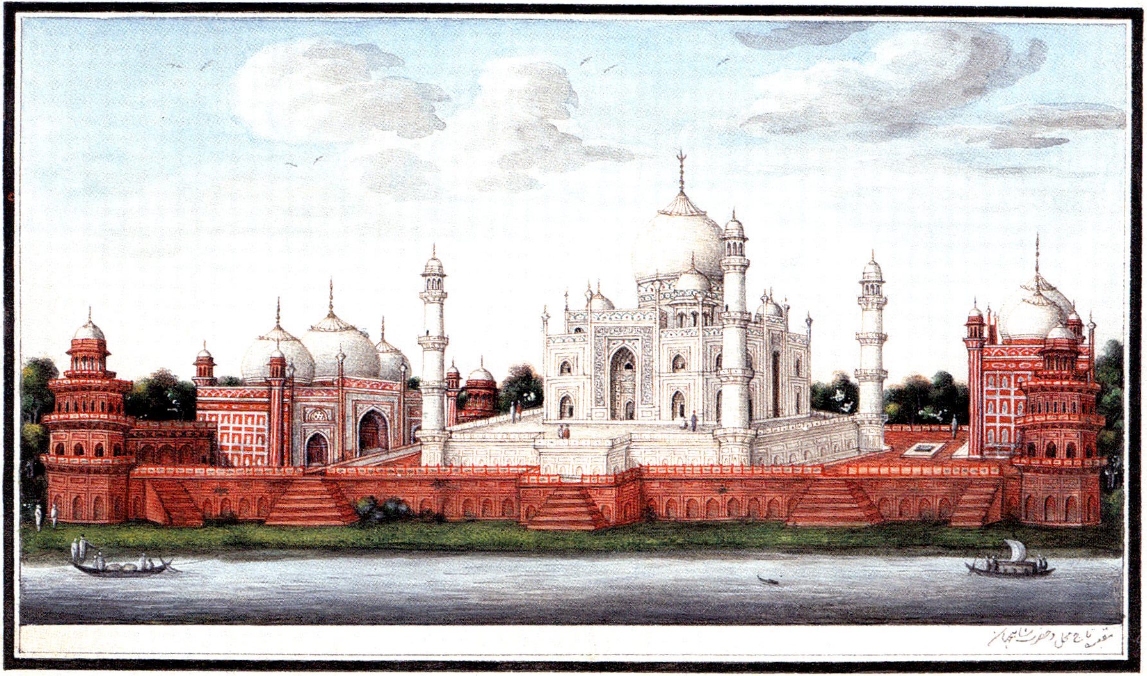
مقبره تاج محل و حضرت شاهجهان

■ The Taj Mahal and the mosques on the side: view from the river, c. 1643

On both sides of the Taj stand two sandstone buildings of which the one to the west of it was originally built as a mosque. It has recesses facing the Kaaba whereas the corresponding one to the east does not. The latter was not intended for prayers and was built primarily to preserve the symmetry of the group. However, it was used as a gathering place for the congregation to assemble before prayers, which were usually held on the death anniversaries of Mumtaz and Shah Jahan.

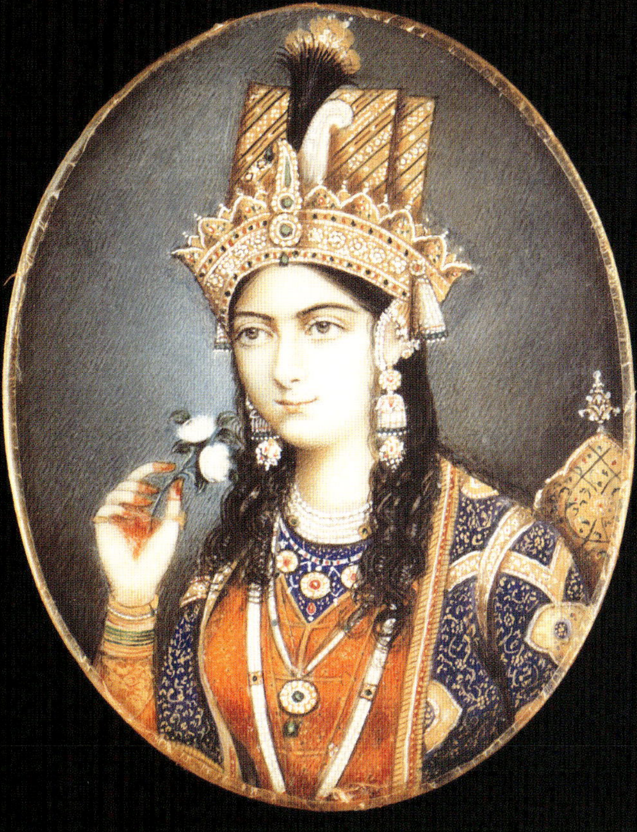

■ Mumtaz Mahal, c. 1592-1631

Mumtaz Mahal or Arjamand Bano (as she was known earlier) is certainly best remembered as Shah Jahan's beloved wife – the inspiration for building the Taj Mahal. It was at their wedding that Shah Jahan gave her the name of Mumtaz Mahal – The Chosen One of the Palace: a name that was to be immortalised in the Taj Mahal.

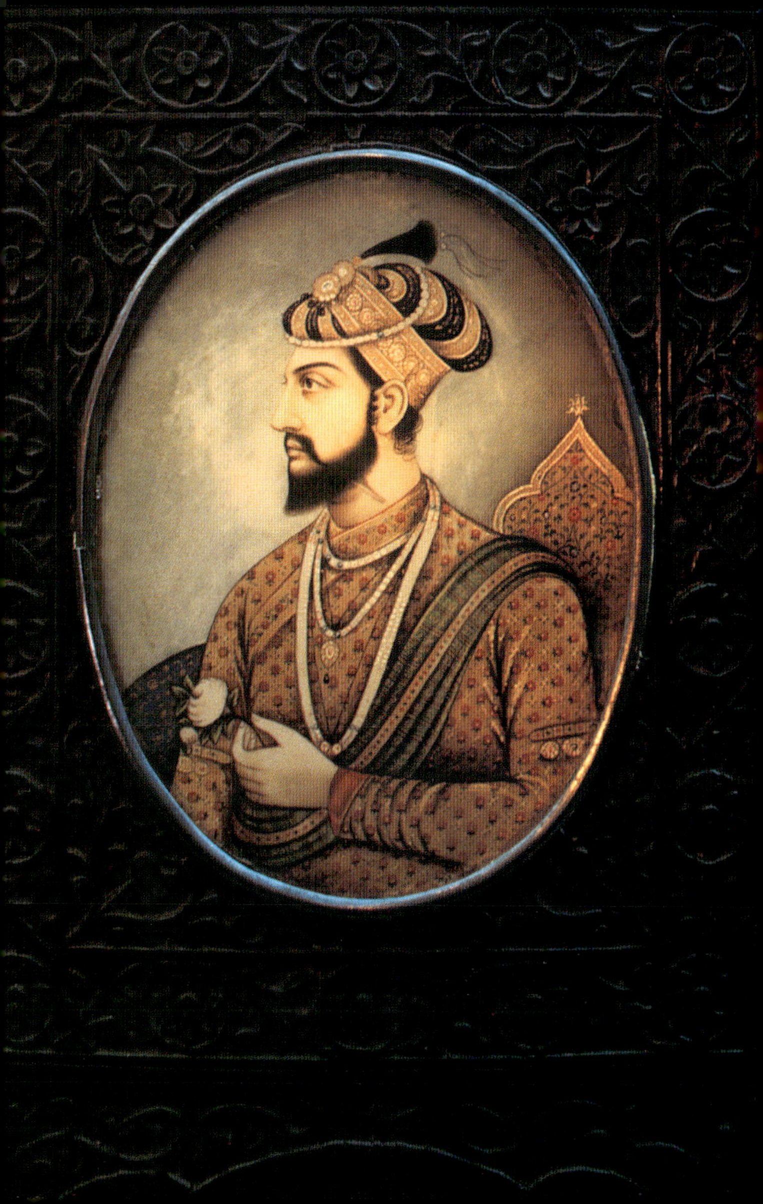

■ Shah Jahan, c. 1592-1660

Shah Jahan is considered to be the greatest builder among the Mughal emperors. Apart from several impressive buildings in the Agra Fort, Shah Jahan's legacy in Agra and in the world is best cherished in the Taj Mahal. Although the imperial court had moved to Delhi and the Emperor spent most of his time there, he often visited the Taj. Thus, his relationship with Agra, which was through the Taj, always had a deep personal meaning for him. He died in 1666, in the Muthumman Burj of the Agra Fort, gazing at the Taj.

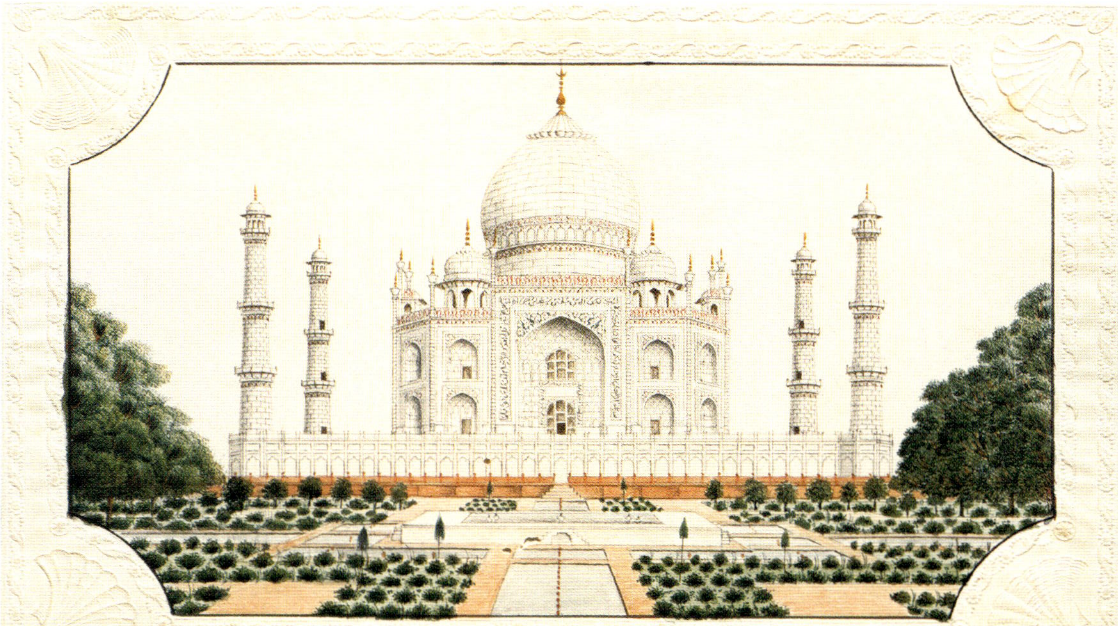

Taj at agra

■ A wide garden view of the Taj Mahal, c. 1643

Since the trees in this picture seem to be short stumps, the view of the Taj Mahal is similar to the way we see it today. The lawns were laid out as part of the restoration work done under Lord Curzon in the early 1900s. It is only after viewing the Taj Mahal from its main gateway in the south that one savours its entire beauty and recapitulates the magical story of its conception. Therein lies its romance.

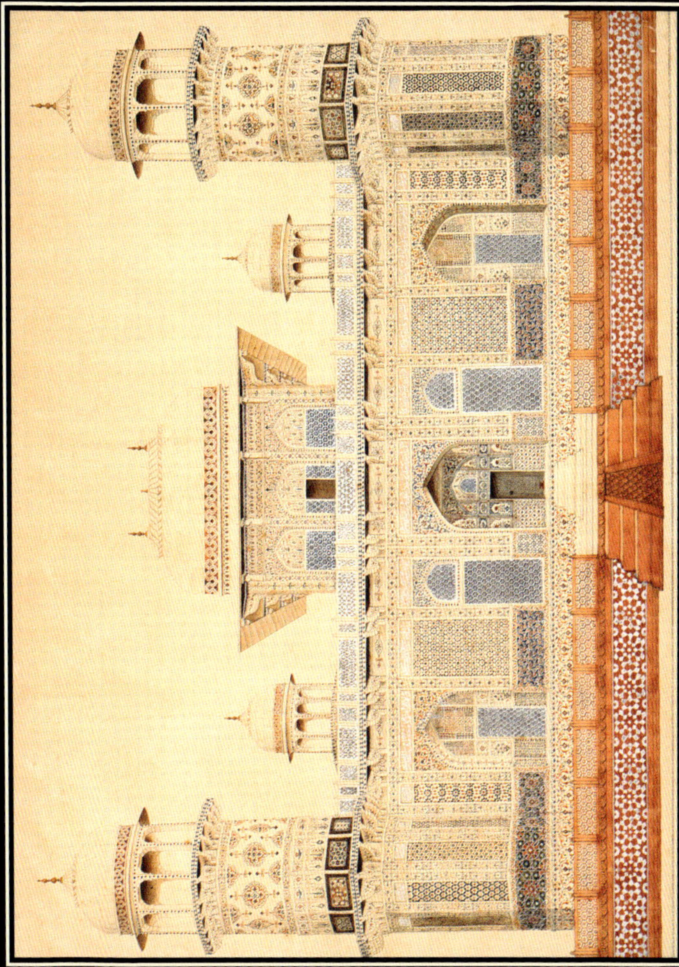

■ Tomb of Itmad-ud-daula, c. 1628

Like Akbar's supremely absurd idea of a copper fort, Noorjahan had conceived of a silver tomb for Itmad-ud-daula but was fortunately convinced by a wise architect that it was a bad idea. Otherwise Agra would have been on the tourist map for being a city of grotesque metal palaces!

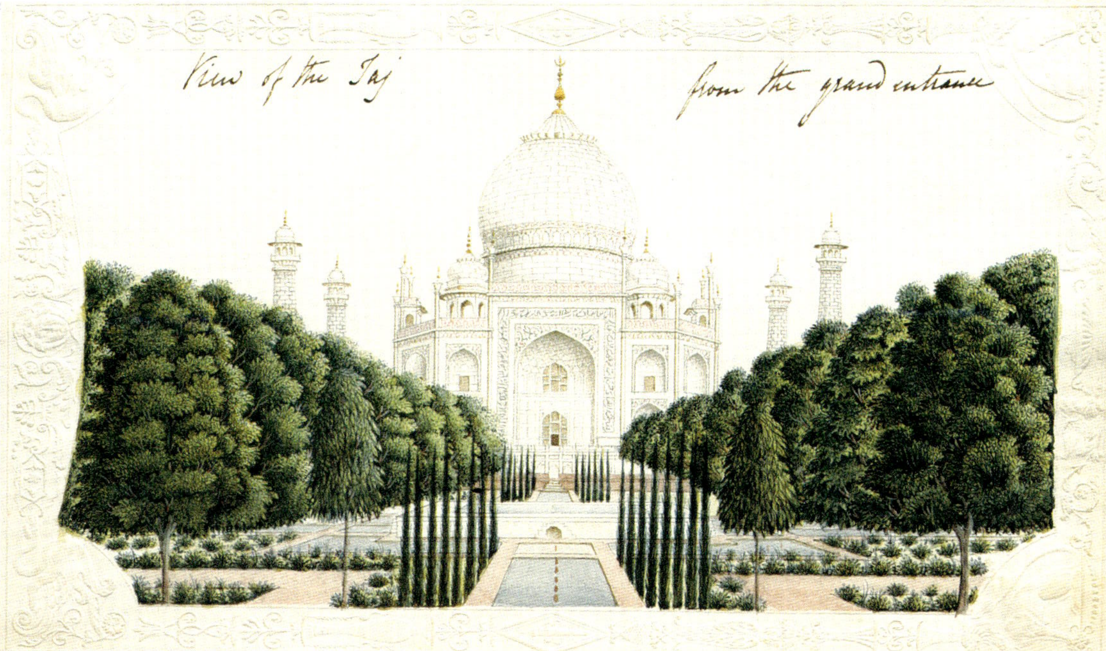
View of the Taj from the grand entrance

■ View of the Taj from the grand entrance, c. 1643

S.A. Latif said of the garden, 'The stately palm, the feathery bamboo, the handsome green banian and the shady orange tree mingle their luxuriant foliage while the odoriferous lemon flowers, roses, jasmine and other fragrant shrubs and plants sweeten the air'. The original Taj garden had a thick cover of fruit and flowering trees, a semblance of which remained till the end of the 19th century. General De Boigne, the French Commander of the Agra Fort in the 19th century, auctioned the fruit – the proceeds of which were used for the maintenance of the complex.

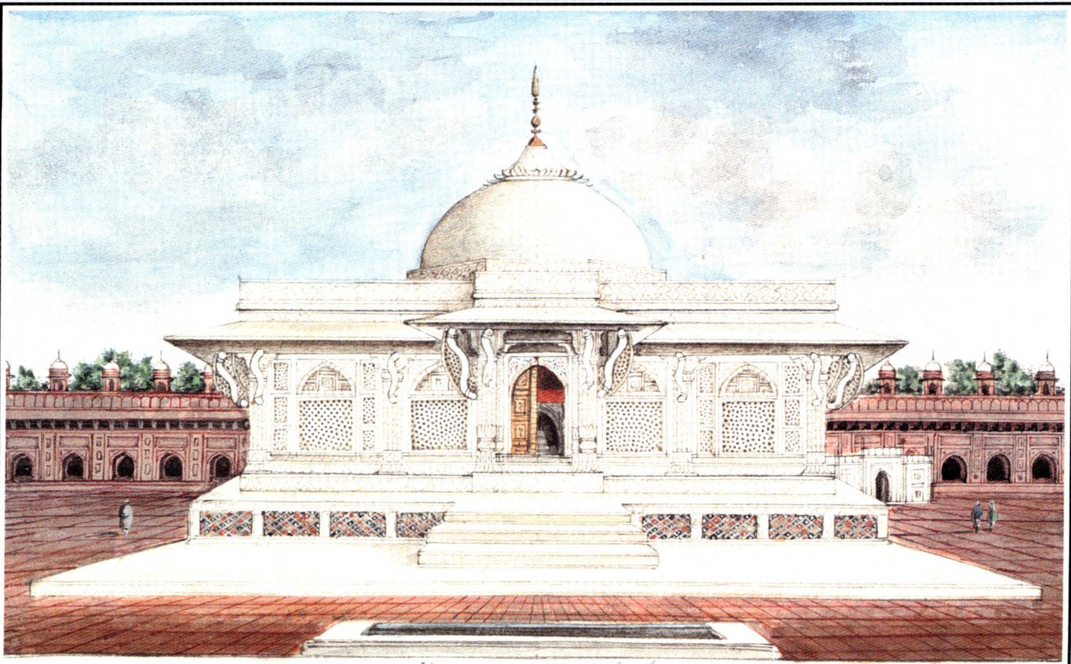

■ Mausoleum of Shaikh Salim Chisti, c. 1570

Shaikh Salim Chisti was Akbar's spiritual mentor and Akbar believed that it was through Chisti's prayers that a long-awaited heir was born to him. After the pir's *(guide) death, Akbar erected a mausoleum for him at Fatehpur Sikri around which he had built his own fort. The original building was of red sandstone; the marble trellis work was added later by Jahangir. These marble* jalis *(lattice-work panels) were the chief ornament of the building. Chisti's mausoleum is one of the finest specimens of Mughal marble buildings pre-dating those of Shah Jahan.*

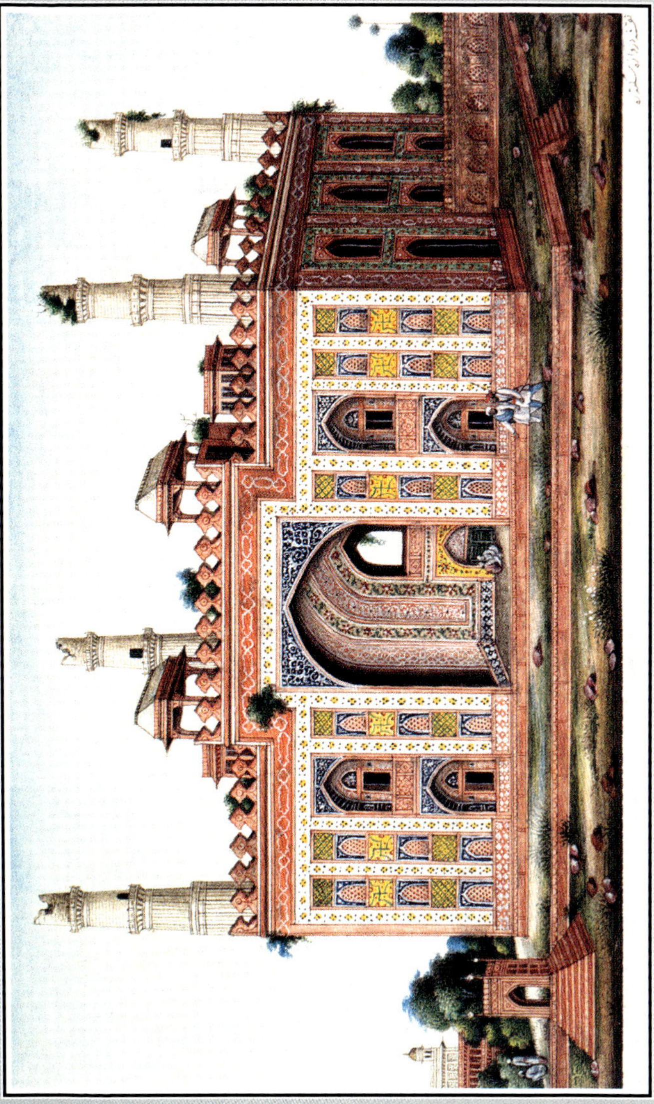

■ Entrance gatehouse to Akbar's mausoleum at Sikandra, c. 1610

The gateway: This impressive building has an entrance befitting its grandeur. It rises to a height of 138 feet and the minarets and stone inlay work that embellish it, were the trendsetters for later Mughal mausoleums.

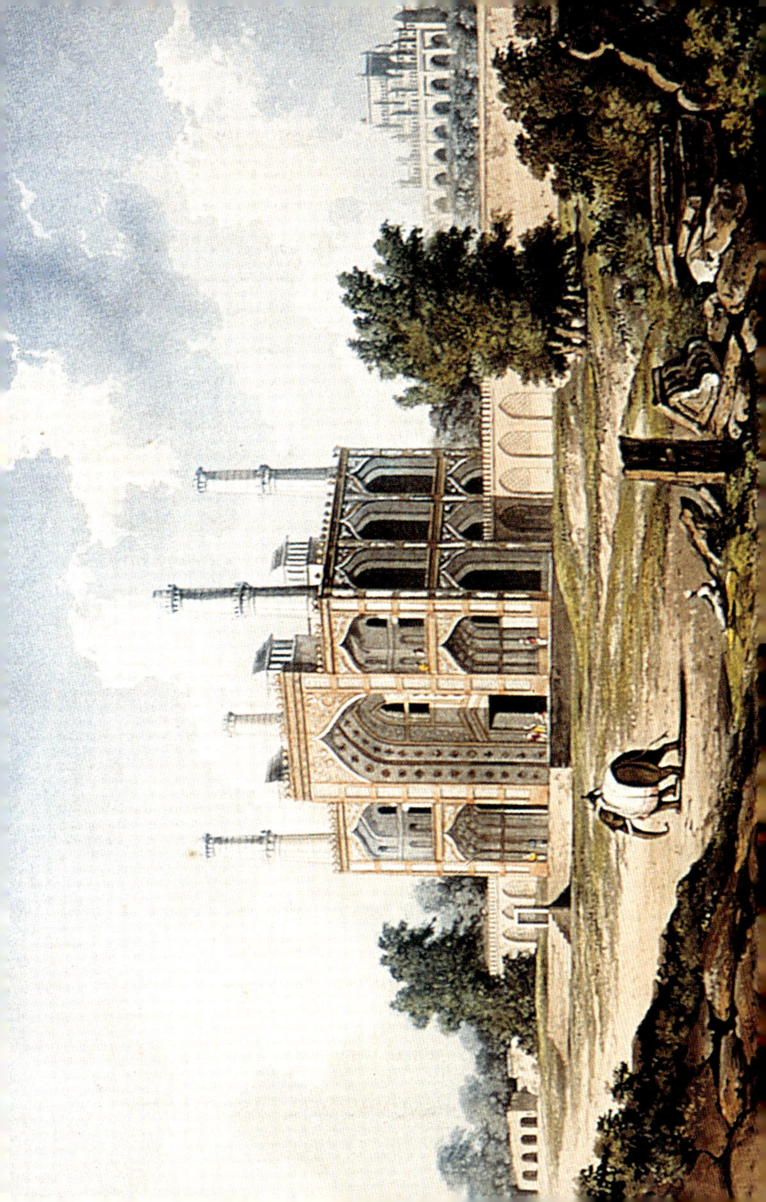

■ Entrance to Akbar's mausoleum at Sikandra, c. 1610

The gateway: Jahangir commissioned the Iranian calligrapher, Abdul Haqq, to design the elaborate calligraphy on the gateway of his father's mausoleum. It is interesting to note that the same man was employed by Shah Jahan later for the same purpose – only this time for the building of the Taj Mahal.

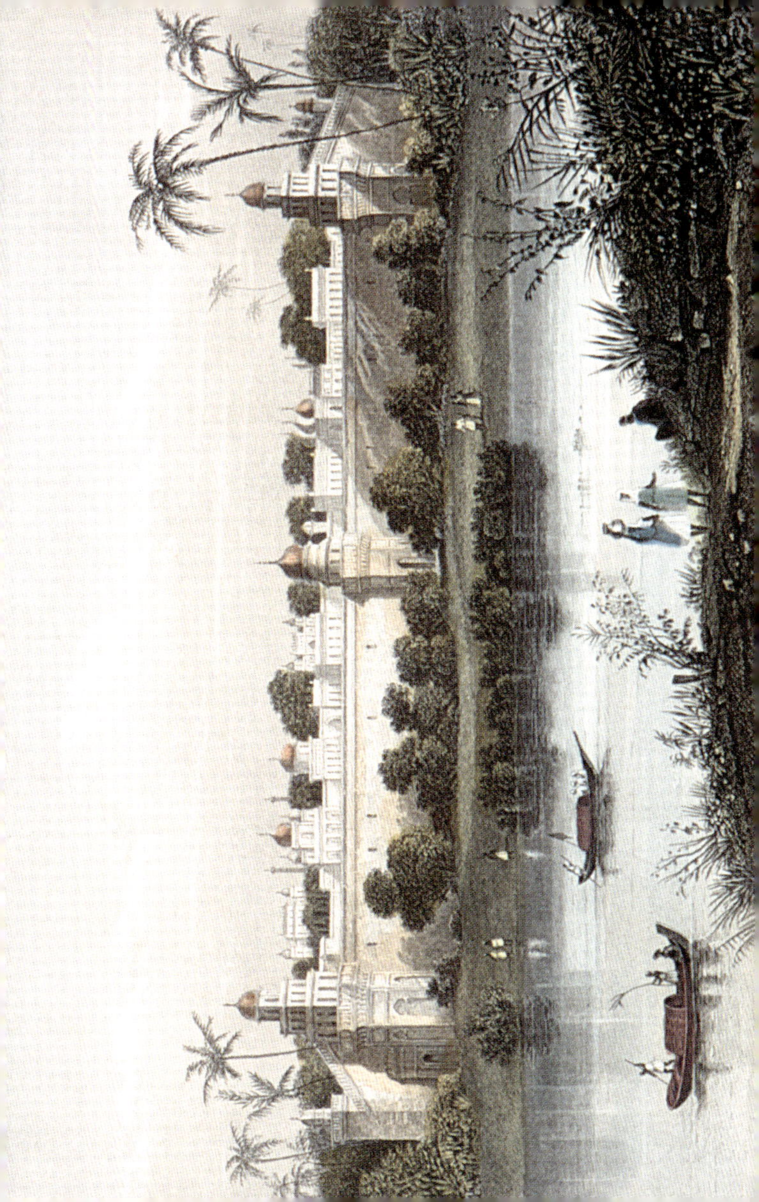

■ The Fort at Agra, c. 1563

This is a most unusual depiction of the red sandstone fort at Agra as having 'white walls'. Apparently a creation of a 19th-century European artist, it was painted at a time when there was a growing interest and appreciation of some Mughal buildings such as the Taj Mahal, Akbar's mausoleum and Itmad-ud-daula. The fort was the seat of government and symbolised power and authority. It was not merely a Mughal 'monument'.

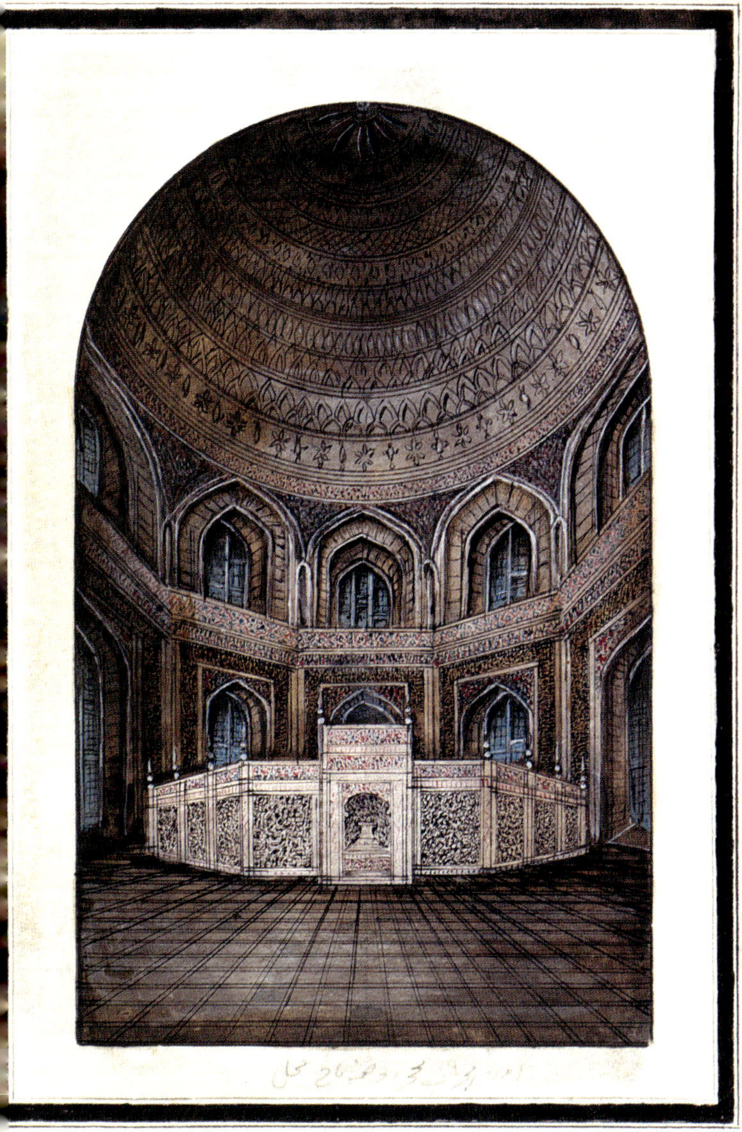

■ Interior of the Taj Mahal, c. 1643

The main octagonal chamber above the graves of the Emperor and Empress has a very beautiful arrangement of light and temperature. Fergusson writes, 'The light in this room is admitted only through a double screen of white marble trellis work of the most exquisite design . . . This was required to temper the glare that otherwise would have been intolerable'.

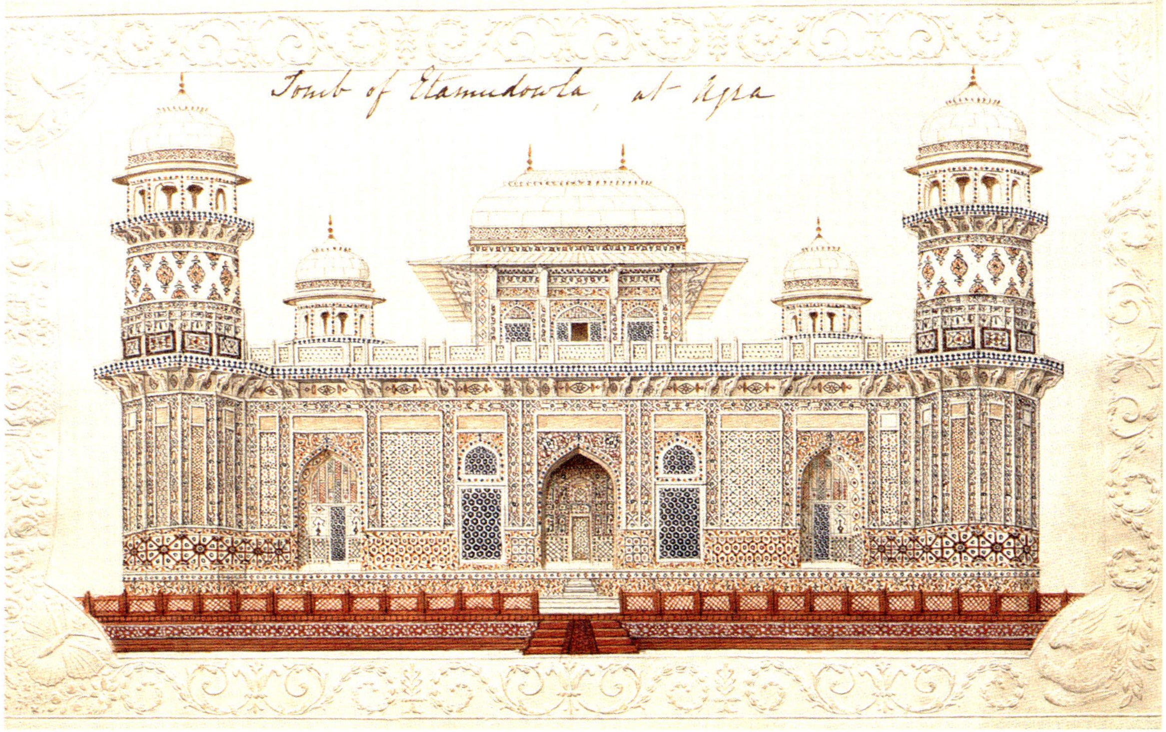
Tomb of Etamudowla, at Agra

■ Mausoleum of Itmad-ud-daula, c. 1628

This is the mausoleum of Itmad-ud-daula, Noorjahan's father. It is significant in that it was one of the first Mughal structures to be built wholly of marble and its exquisite inlay work was seen for the first time in such profusion.

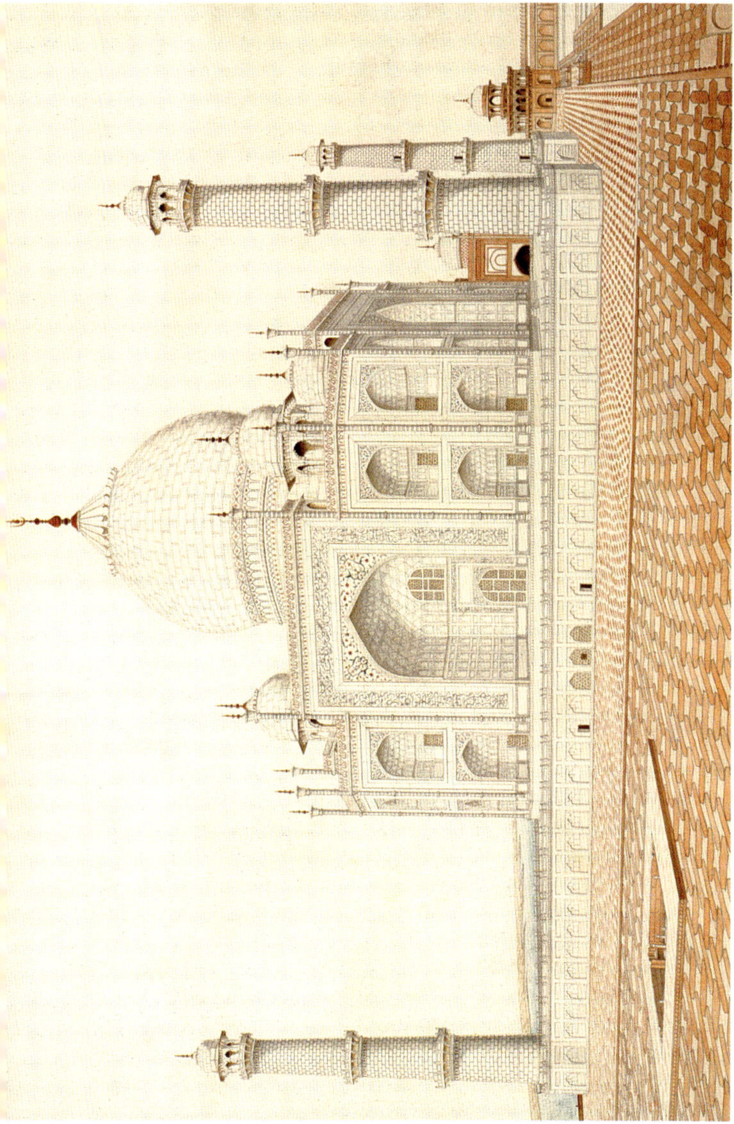

■ The Taj and a part of its courtyard, c. 1643

The courtyard to the west of the Taj Mahal was a part of the mosque and its floor was marked off into small portions, each big enough for one person to stand or sit on during prayer. The corresponding courtyard of the Jamaat Khana was, in the centuries to follow, put to a more secular use or rather misuse. Several of the British officials and Indian princes used it as a venue for lavish balls and parties in the 19th century.

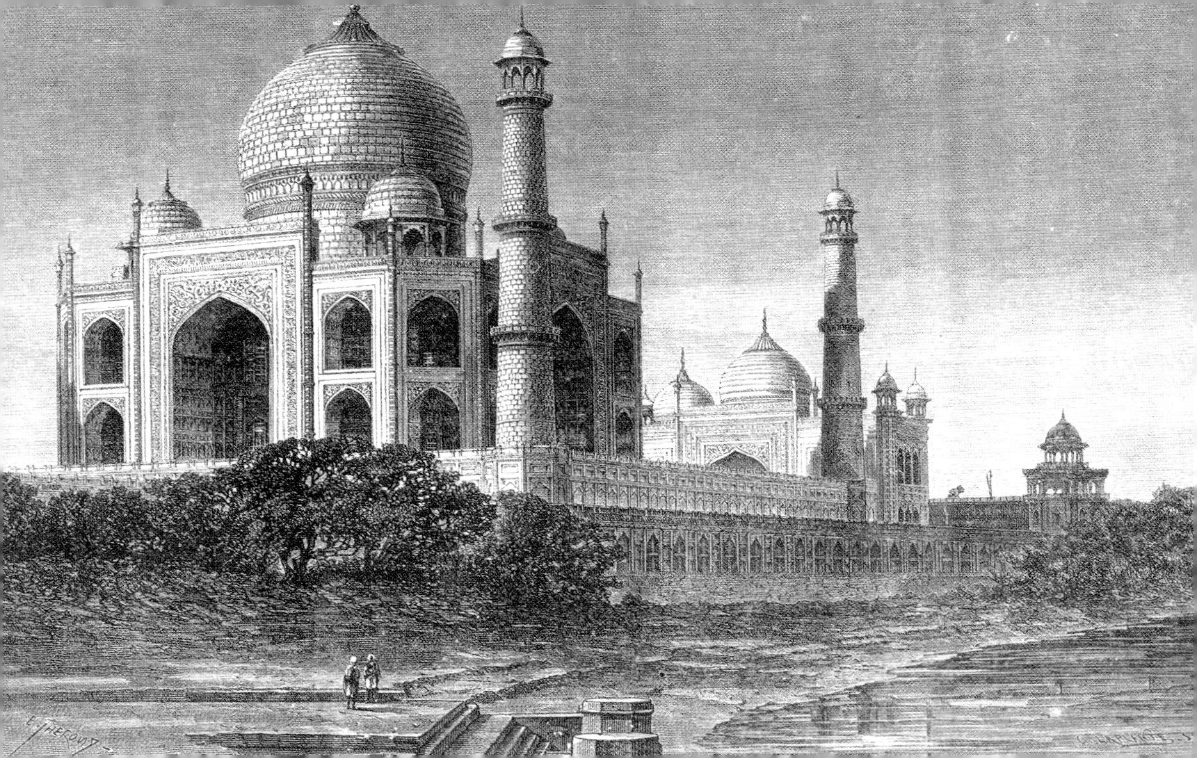

■ General view of the Taj Mahal, c. 1643

A contemporary writer, Miss Gordon Cumming, describes the Taj Mahal in almost poetical language as a cluster of pearly, snow-white domes nestling round one grand central dome, like a gigantic pearl; all these crowning a building of purest, highly-polished marble, so perfect in its proportions, so lovely in its design, so restful to the eye, and so simple yet so complex in its simplicity, that it resembles rather the marble embodiment of a fairy dream than any work of human hands.

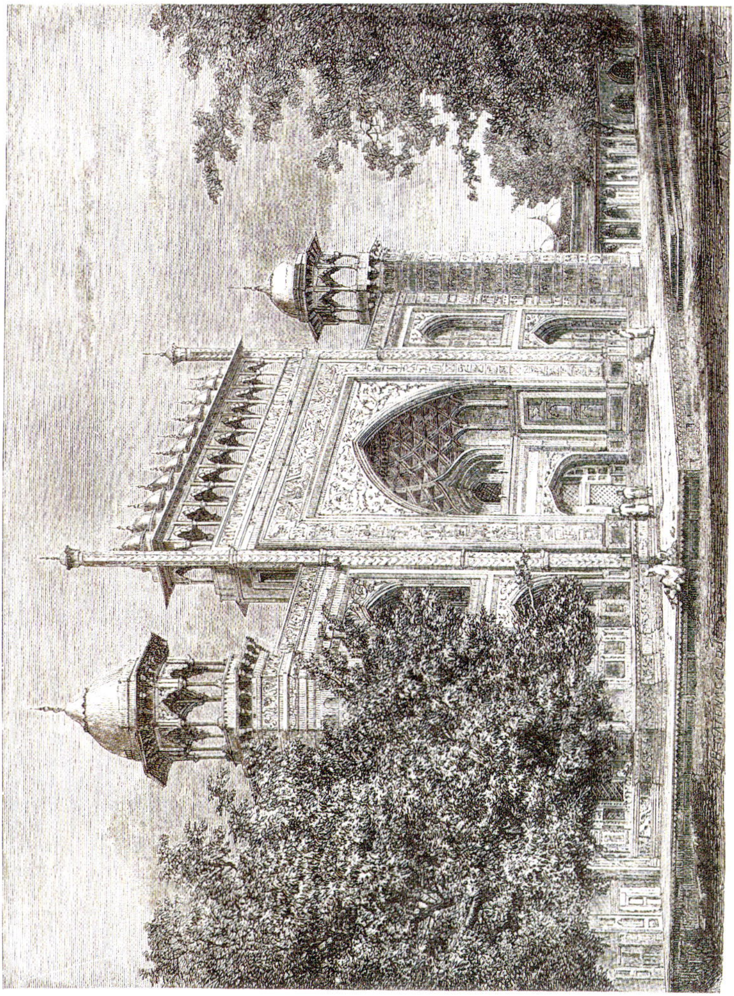

■ Gate of the gardens of the Taj Mahal, c. 1643

A wall of red sandstone, about 60 feet high, encloses the entire area, a space of nearly 40 acres, and separates it from the river. This wall is finely covered with large groups and clusters of flowers, inlaid with pure white marble, and adorned with beautifully wrought niches.

■ *Front cover:* Interior of the Taj Mahal, c. 1643

■ *Pages 2-3:* The Taj Mahal framed in arches, c. 1643

■ *Back cover:* Mumtaj Mahal, c. 1592-1631